Songs, rhymes and stories by Jean Bunton

4

Contents

Unit	Letter(s)	Sound(s)	Page
1	ir/ear	/ɜːr/	1
2	air	/er/	3
3	ear/eer	/ɪr/	5
Review 1			7
4	bl & pl	/bl/ & /pl/	9
5	cl & gl	/kl/ & /gl/	11
6	fl & sl	/fl/ & /sl/	13
7	br & pr	/br/ & /pr/	15
8	cr, fr & gr	/kr/, /fr/ & /gr/	17
9	dr & tr	/dr/ & /tr/	19
Review 2			21
10	sc/sk	/sk/	23
11	sm & sn	/sm/ & /sn/	25
12	sp & st	/sp/ & /st/	27
13	sw	/sw/	29
Review 3			31
14	tw	/tw/	33
15	qu	/kw/	35
16	c & g	/s/ & /dʒ/	37
Review 4			39
Phonics Dictionary			41

1

ir/ear

Listen to these words.

 ir

1.
b**ir**d

3.
sh**ir**t

5.
th**ir**ty

 ear

2.
Earth

4.
s**ear**ch

6.
early

Say the rhyme.

"Thank you."

The th**ir**sty b**ir**d arrived **ear**ly
To s**ear**ch for food and a drink.
He tapped three times on my window
To wake me up **ear**ly, I think.
I gave him a dish of water.
He said "thank you"
And gave me a wink.

 Act the rhyme.

Listen to these words.

1 **ch**air

2 **f**air

3 **h**air

4 **p**air

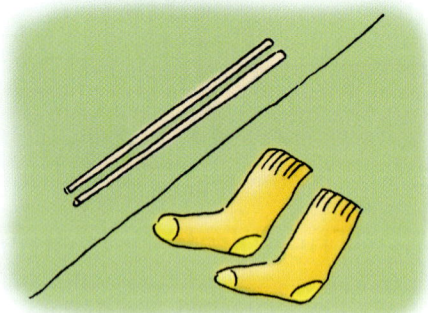

5 **st**airs

6 **air**port

Say the rhyme.

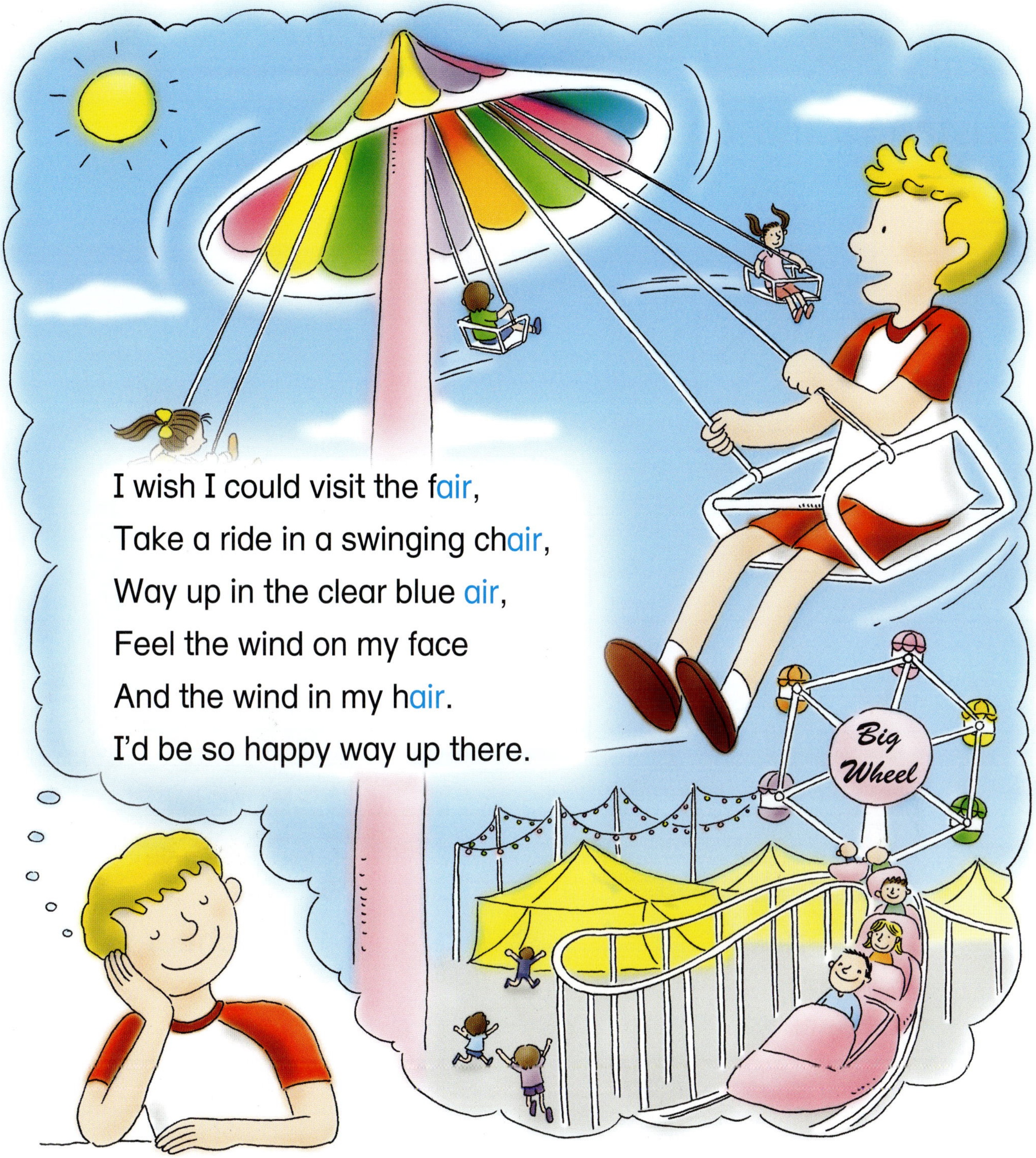

I wish I could visit the fair,
Take a ride in a swinging chair,
Way up in the clear blue air,
Feel the wind on my face
And the wind in my hair.
I'd be so happy way up there.

ACTIVITY **Which ride do you like?**

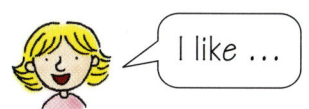

3 ear/eer

Listen to these words.

ear

1
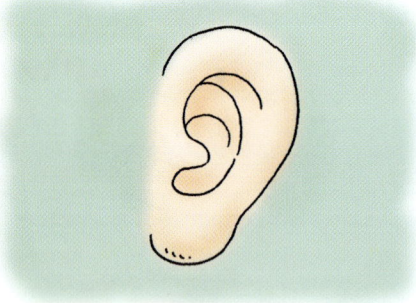
ear

eer

2

beer

3

near

4

cheer

5

year

6

deer

Read the letter.

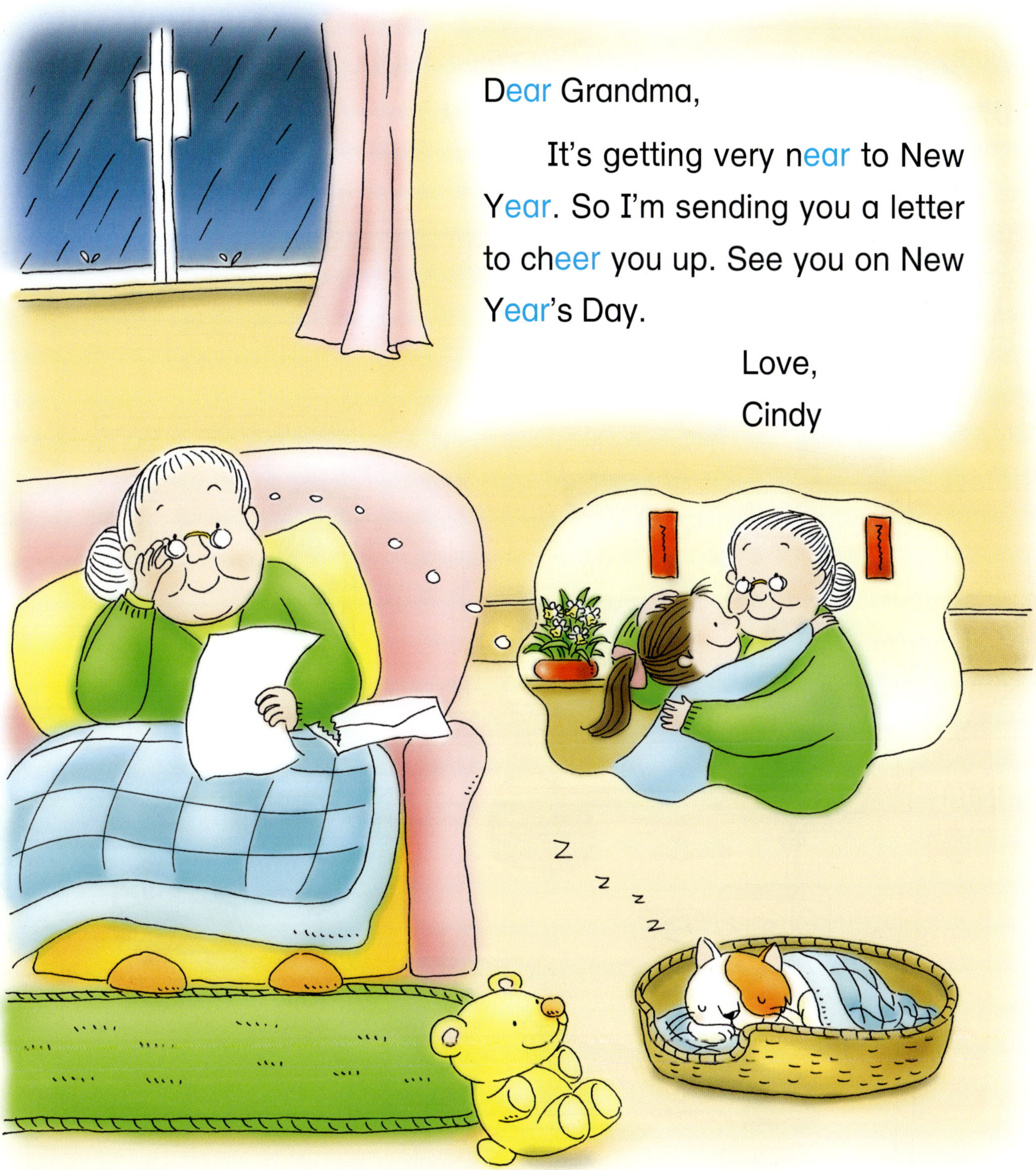

Dear Grandma,

It's getting very near to New Year. So I'm sending you a letter to cheer you up. See you on New Year's Day.

Love,
Cindy

ACTIVITY Think of someone dear to you. Write another letter.

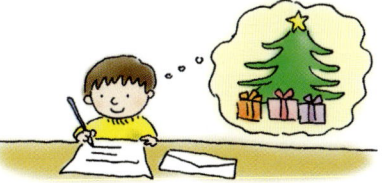

Review 1

Play the game. Say the correct words for the pictures.
Draw the route for each child.

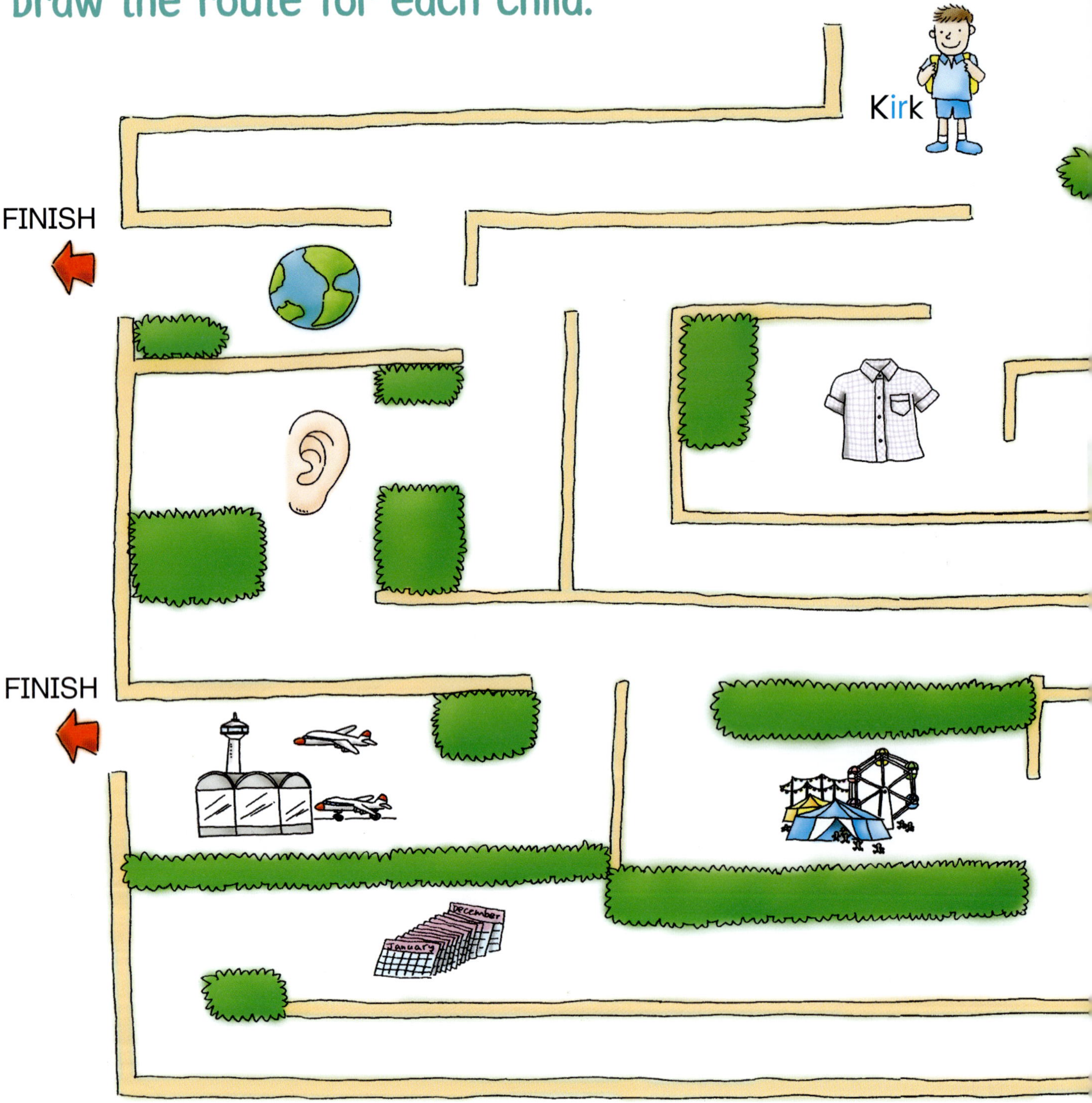

Kirk

FINISH

 air

 ear/eer

Claire   Meara

FINISH

8

Listen to these words.

bl

pl

1

blind

2
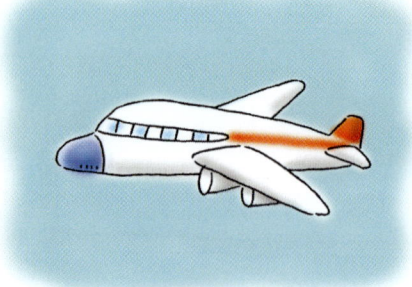
plane

3

block

4

plate

5
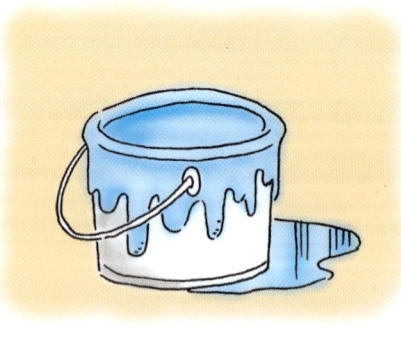
blue

6

plenty

Sing the song.

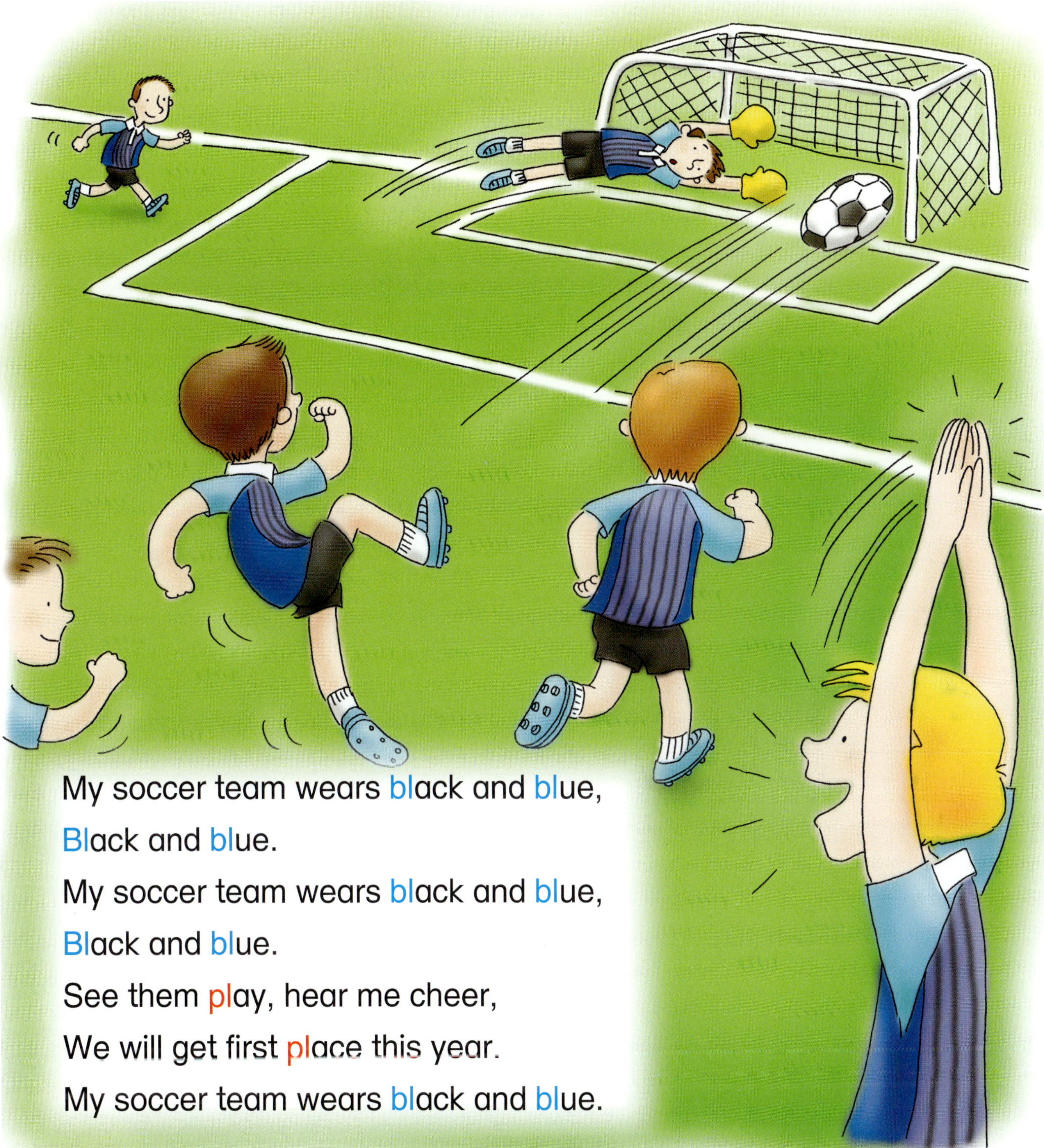

My soccer team wears black and blue,
Black and blue.
My soccer team wears black and blue,
Black and blue.
See them play, hear me cheer,
We will get first place this year.
My soccer team wears black and blue.

ACTIVITY **Design a uniform for a soccer team.**

Listen to these words.

cl

1
clean

3
climb

5
clock

gl

2
glass

4
glide

6
glove

Read the story.

1

Yesterday I forgot to wear my glasses.

2

I couldn't see the clock clearly.

3

I was late for class.

4

I'm glad I've got my glasses on today.

 What else did the boy forget?

Listen to these words.

fl

1

fly

3

floor

5

flower

sl

2

sleep

4
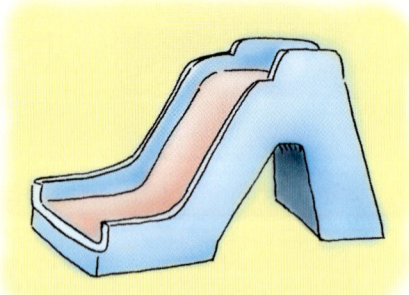
slide

6

slow

Read the story.

1 I am learning to ski. **Sl**owly I stand up.

2 Now I can **sl**ide down.

3 I **sl**ide faster and faster ... I can almost **fl**y.

4 Oh, no! It's very **sl**ippery. I fall **fl**at on the **fl**oor!

 Act the story.

Listen to these words.

br

1

break

3

brown

5

brother

pr

2

prawn

4

price

6

present

Read the story.

My brother is a hall monitor at school. He is bright and brave.

He has soccer practice every day and hopes to win the first prize again.

Everybody praises my brother. I'm really proud of him.

Act the story.

Listen to these words.

 1

crab

2

cry

 3

fridge

4

fruit

 5

grass

6

green

Say the sentences.

Don't cry!
If you eat too much ice cream,
You will grow fatter.
But if you eat fresh green fruit,
You will grow taller than the fridge.

What else can we do to grow taller?

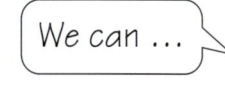

We can ...

Listen to these words.

dr

1
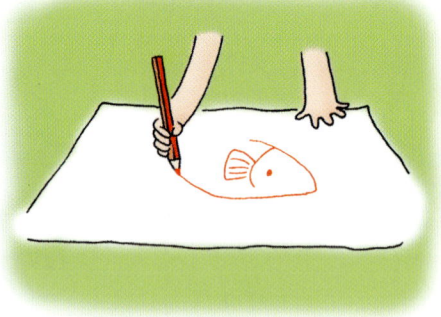
draw

tr

2

train

3

drink

4

tram

5

dry

6

tree

Read the story.

I dream about driving a car. I dream about making a trip to the park. I can take lots of food and drink.

If the weather is hot and dry, I can stop driving and have a picnic under a tree.

 What do you dream about?
Draw and tell your friend.

Review 2

bl pl cl gl fl sl

Say the words.

1
block
clock

2
bridge
fridge

3
cream
green

4
drain
train

5
drawer
floor

6
flies
fries

7
glass
grass

8
glide
slide

9
play
pray

br pr cr fr gr dr tr

Choose and write nine words from page 21. Play bingo.

1. _____	2. _____	3. _____
4. _____	5. _____	6. _____
7. _____	8. _____	9. _____

sc/sk

Listen to these words.

sc   sk

1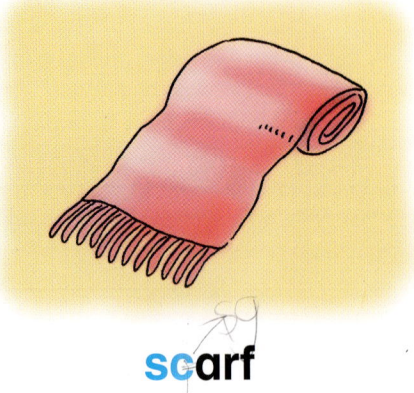
scarf

2
skate

3
score

4
skirt

5
Scout

6
sky

23

Sing the song.

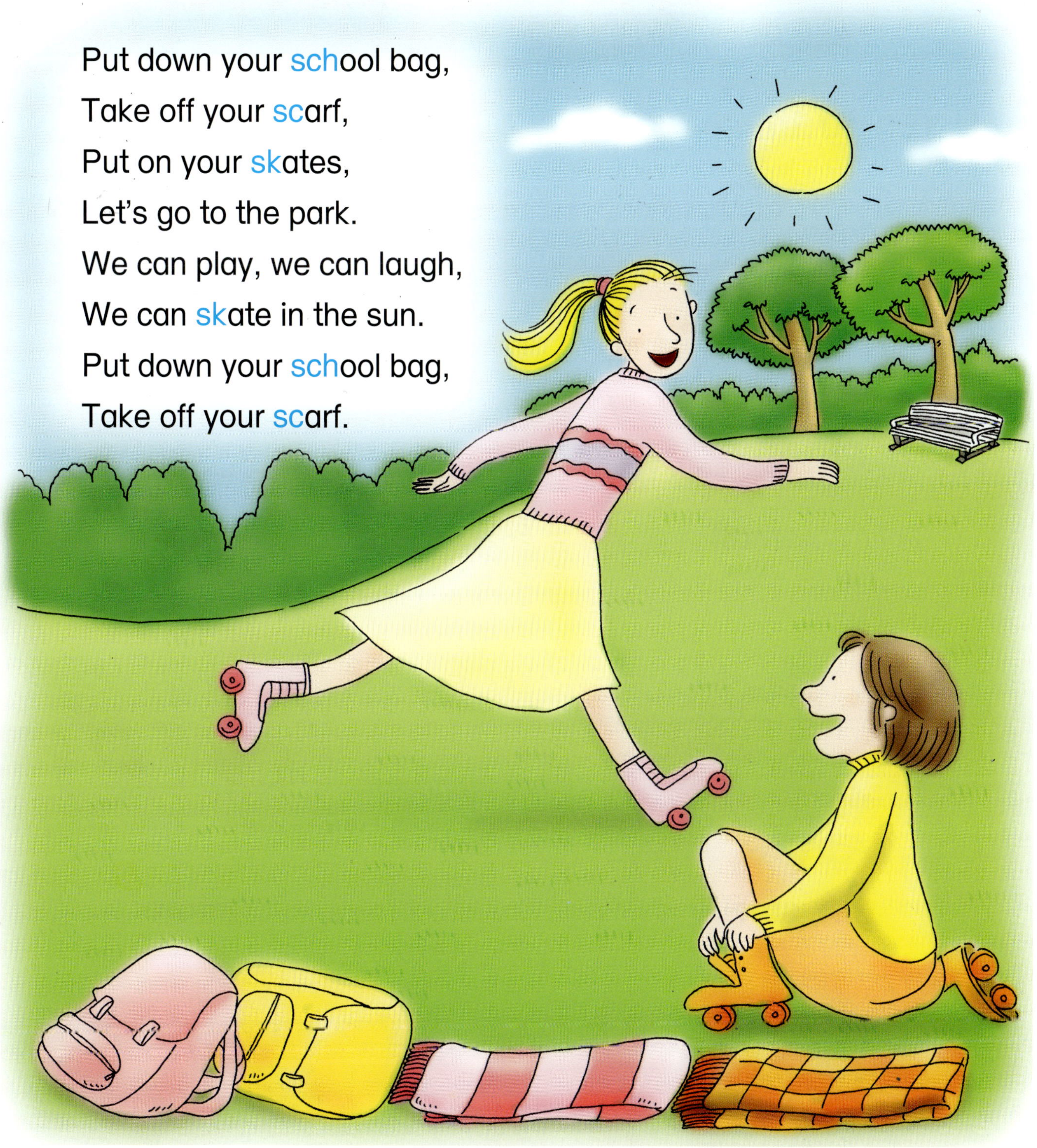

Put down your school bag,
Take off your scarf,
Put on your skates,
Let's go to the park.
We can play, we can laugh,
We can skate in the sun.
Put down your school bag,
Take off your scarf.

 Act the song.

Listen to these words.

sm

1
small

2
snake

sn

3
smell

4
snore

5
smooth

6
snow

Say the rhyme.

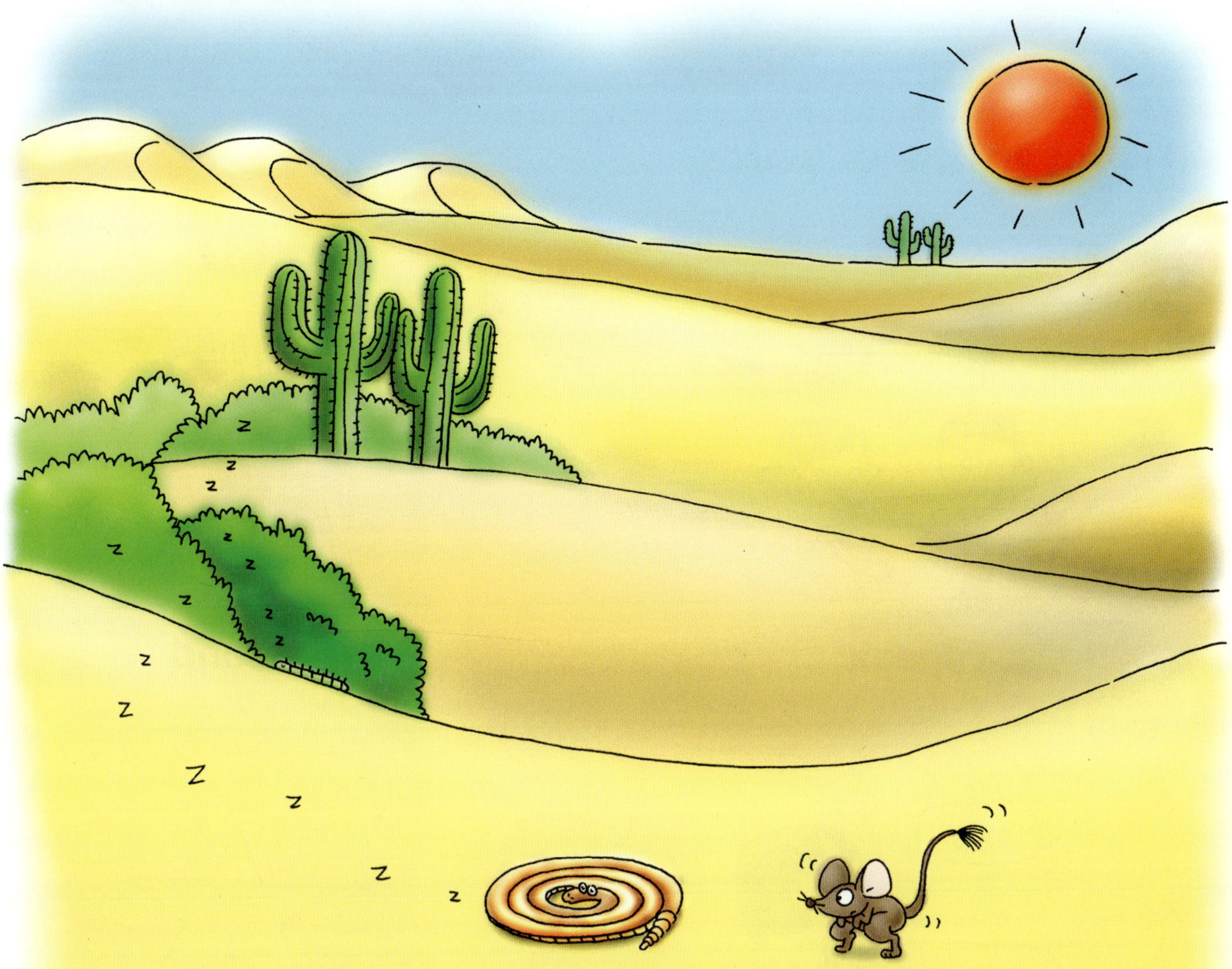

Can you see the small brown snake
Sleeping in the sun?
Can you see its smooth long shape
Sleeping in the sun?
Can you hear the snake snoring,
Sleeping in the sun?

What can you find in the bush? Say another rhyme.

Listen to these words.

1.
speak

2.
stand

3.
spell

4.
star

5.
sports

6.
stop

Say the rhyme.

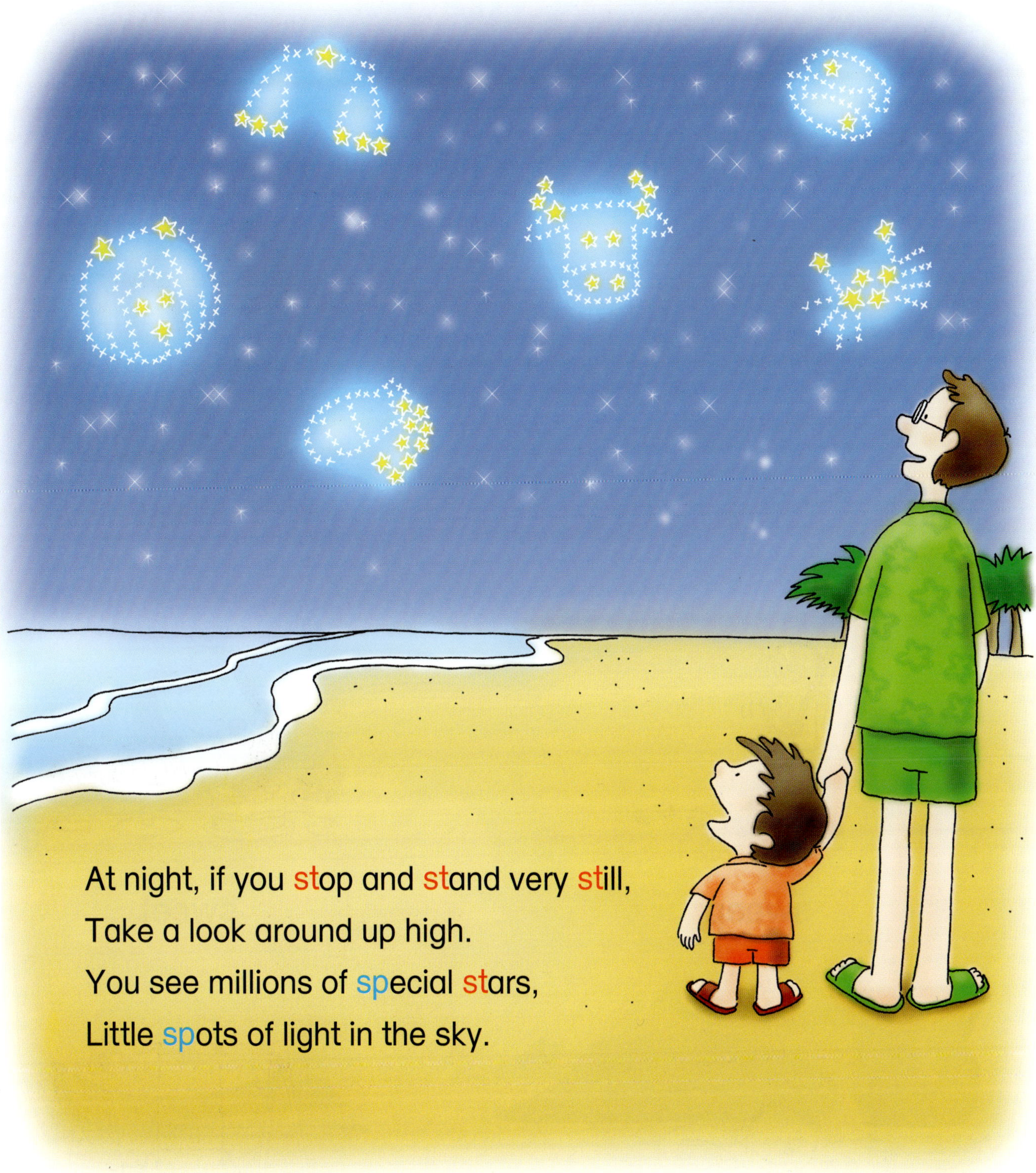

At night, if you stop and stand very still,
Take a look around up high.
You see millions of special stars,
Little spots of light in the sky.

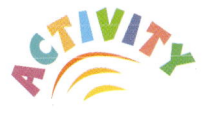

ACTIVITY Which star do you like most? Why? Point and say.

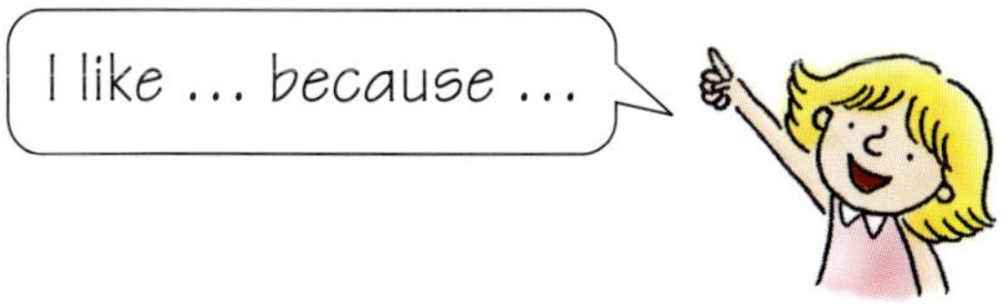
I like ... because ...

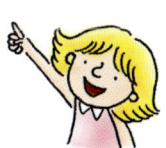

Listen to these words.

1

swan

2

sweat

3

sweep

4

sweet

5

swim

6
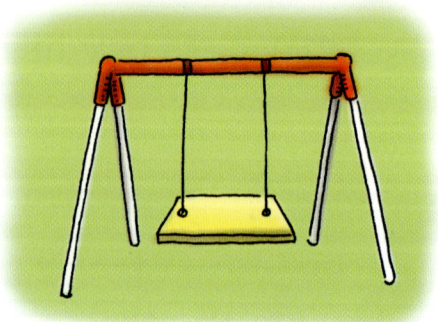
swing

Read the story.

1. I can swim like a swan.

2. I can swing in the trees like a monkey.

3. I can sing a sweet song like a bird.

4. But I have to sweep the floor!

 Act the girl.

Review 3

Play the game. Say the correct words for the pictures or words with the beginning letters.

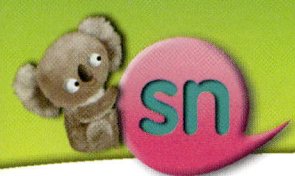

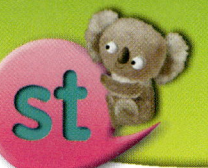

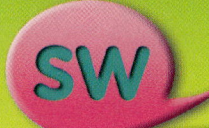

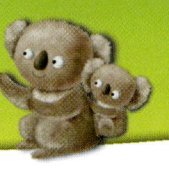

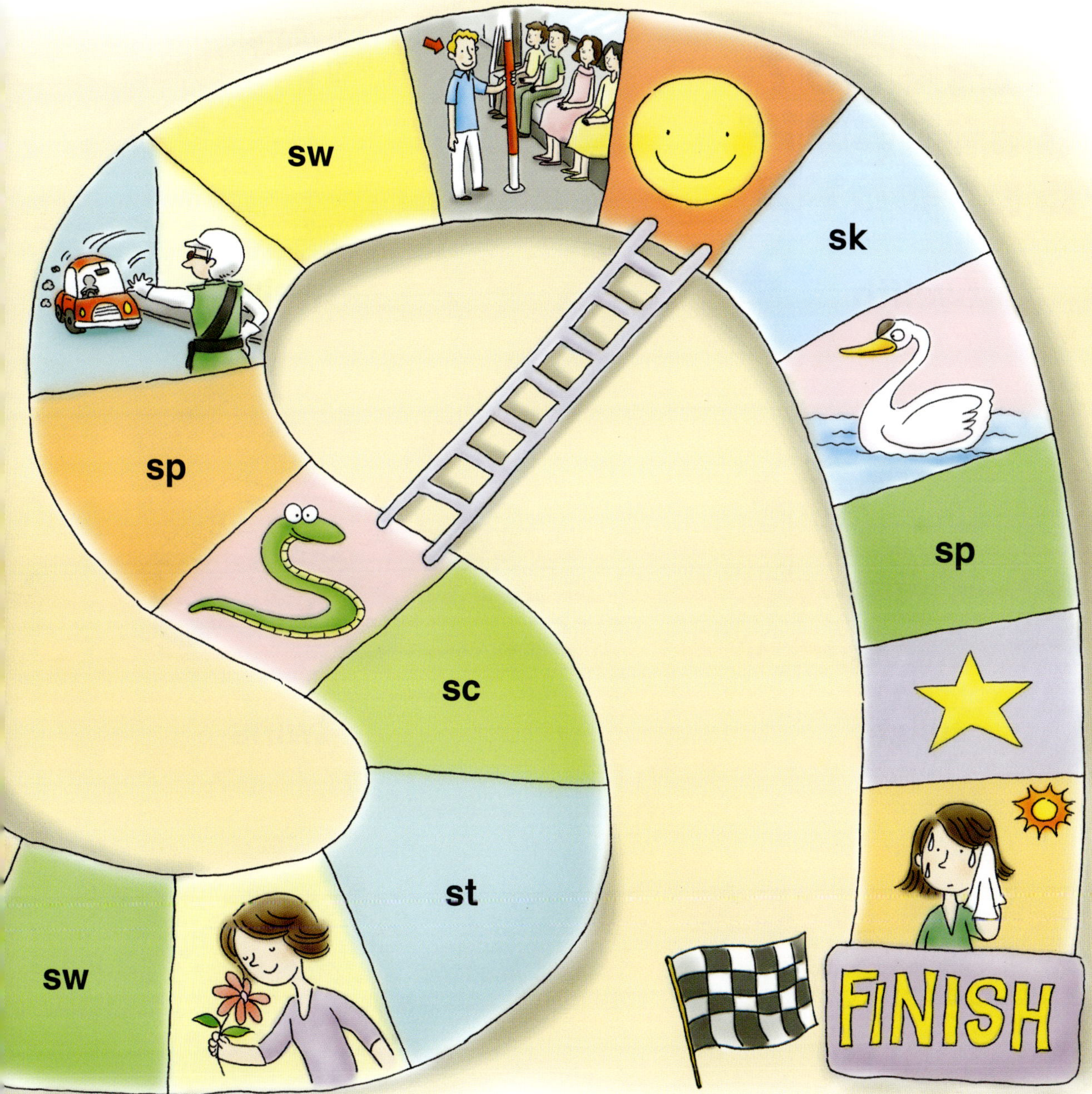
sw
st
sc
sp
sw
sk
sp
FINISH

Listen to these words.

1

twelfth

2

twelve

3

twice

4

twins

5
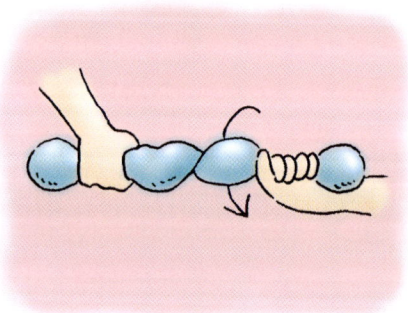
twist

6

twenty

Say the sentences.

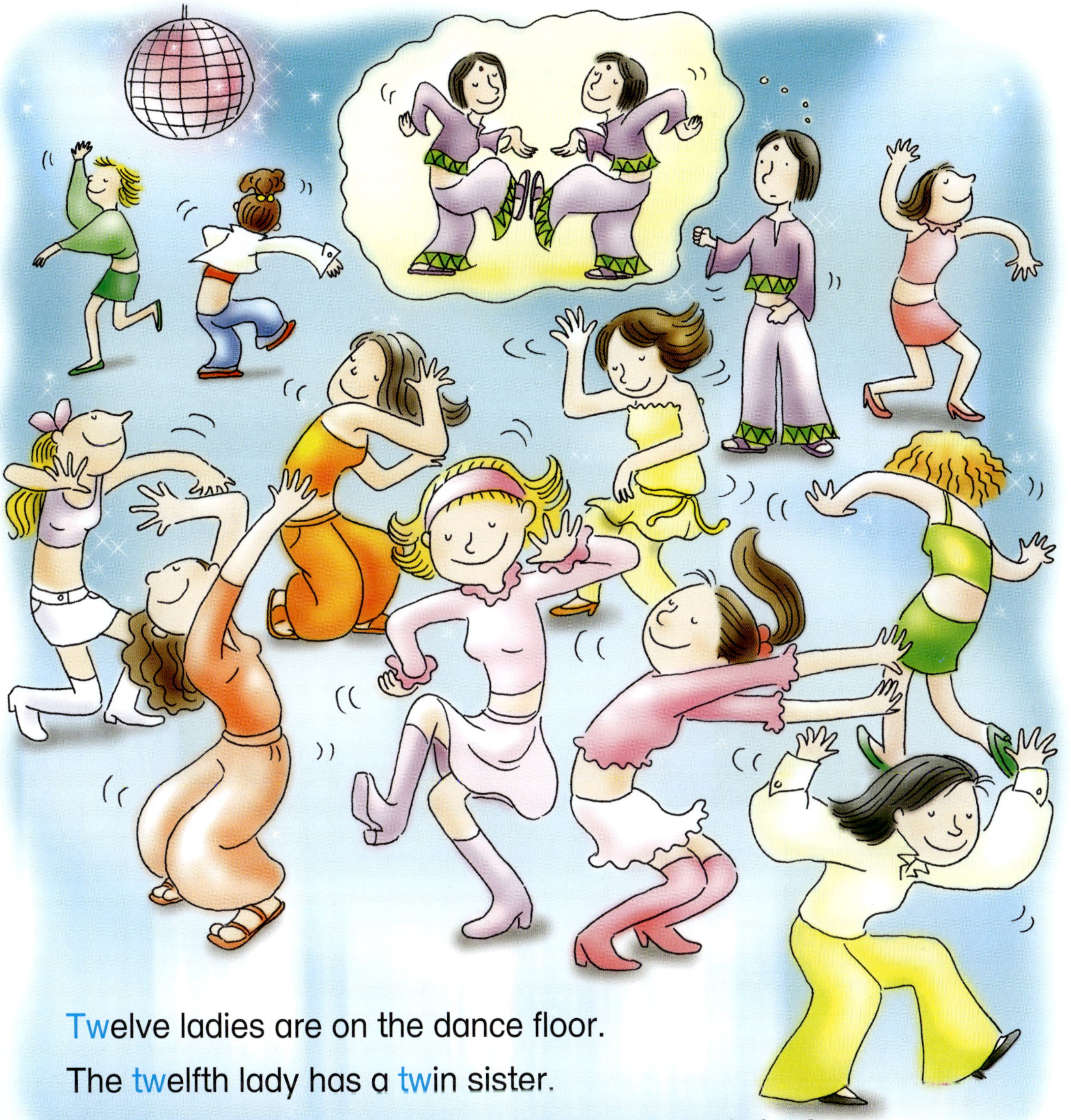

Twelve ladies are on the dance floor.
The twelfth lady has a twin sister.
Do you think the twins will have twice as much fun?

Can you answer the question above?

Listen to these words.

1

queen

2

quick

3

quiet

4

quiz

5

quarter

6

question

Say the rhyme.

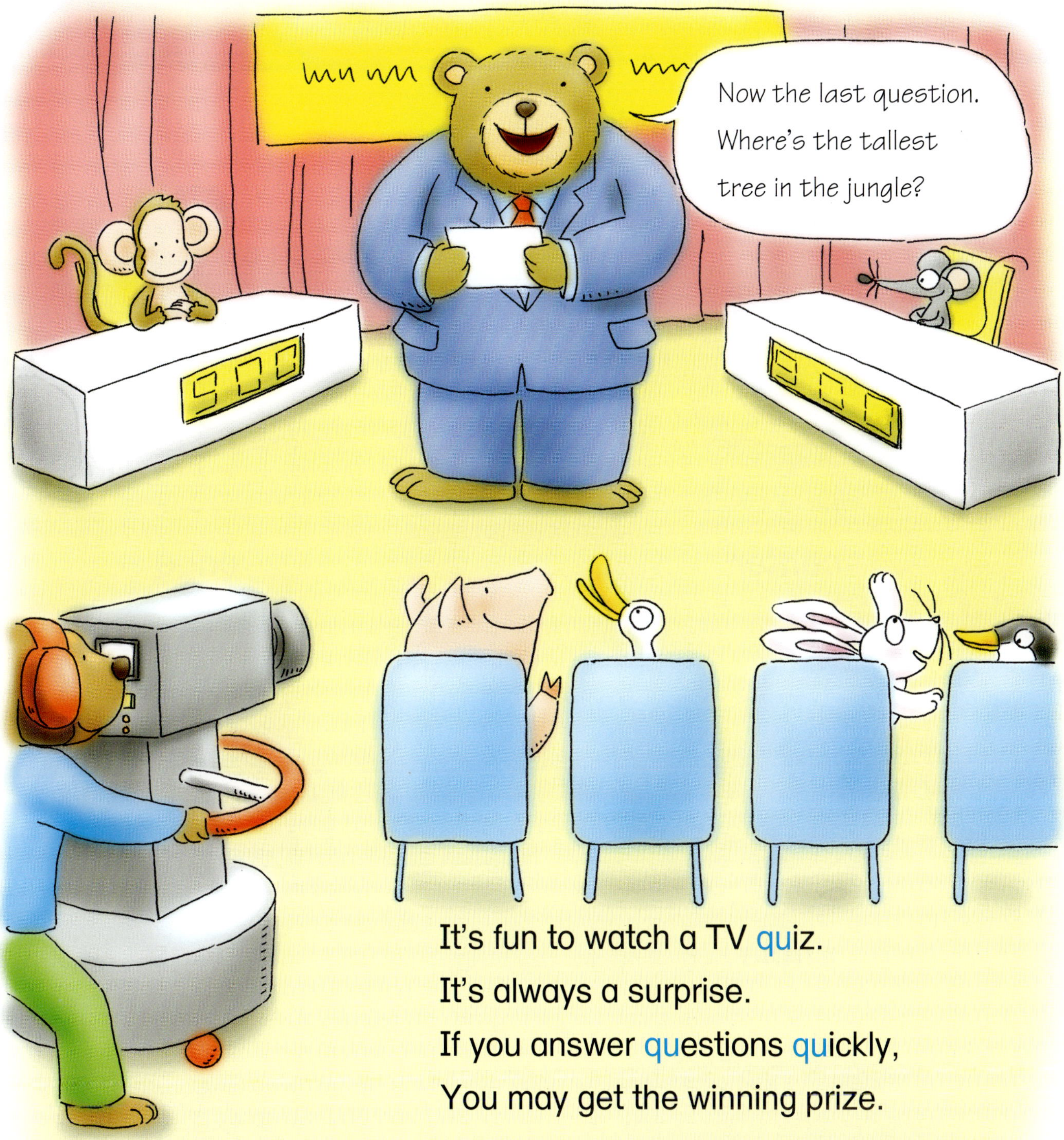
Now the last question. Where's the tallest tree in the jungle?

It's fun to watch a TV **qu**iz.
It's always a surprise.
If you answer **qu**estions **qu**ickly,
You may get the winning prize.

ACTIVITY **Who do you think may win the quiz?**

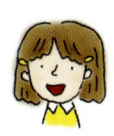

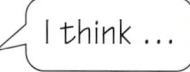

I think ...

Listen to these words.

c

1
center

3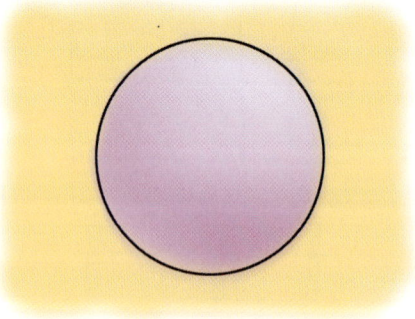
circle

5
cycle

g

2
ca**g**e

4
ju**dg**e

6
gin**g**er

Say the sentences.

The park in the city center is large.
It has a huge bridge.
You can run. You can jog.
But you can't cycle.
It's a pity there's no cycle path.

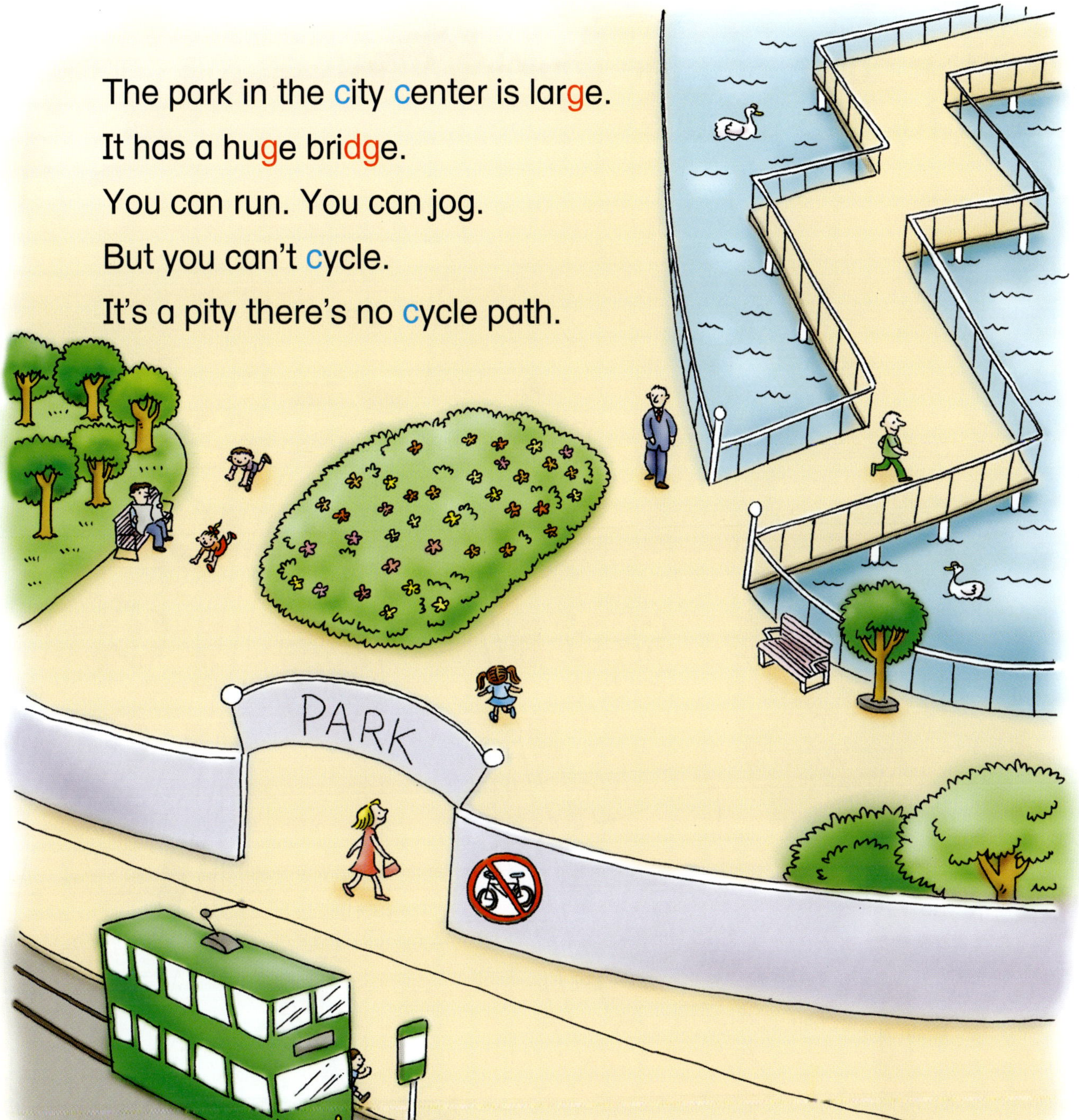

Is there a park near your school?
What is there in the park?

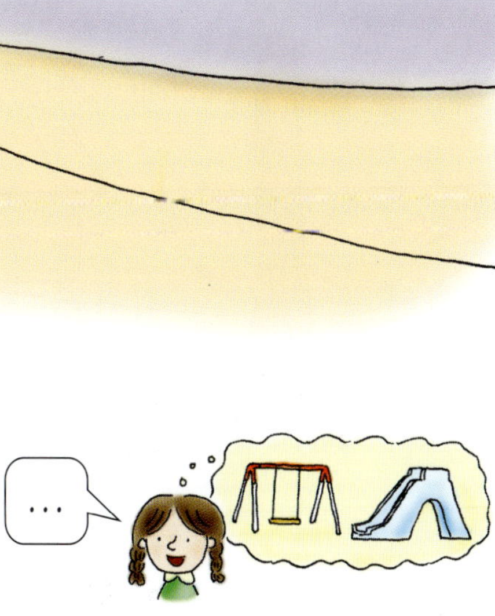

Review 4

Play the game. Say the rhyming words or the correct words for the pictures.

 c  g   more ...

spell
third
plate
free
dirty
FINISH

Phonics

ir ear	b**ir**d 	sh**ir**t 	th**ir**ty 	**Ear**th 	s**ear**ch 	**ear**ly 
air	ch**air** 	f**air** 	h**air** 	p**air** 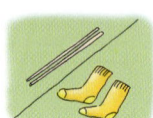	st**air**s 	**air**port 
ear eer	**ear** 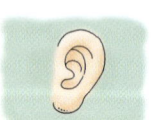	n**ear** 	y**ear** 	b**eer** 	ch**eer** 	d**eer** 
bl pl	**bl**ind 	**bl**ock 	**bl**ue 	**pl**ane 	**pl**ate 	**pl**enty 

Dictionary

	 	 	 	 		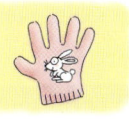

cl / gl — clean, climb, clock, glass, glide, glove

     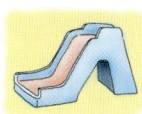 

fl / sl — fly, floor, flower, sleep, slide, slow

br / pr — break, brown, brother, prawn, price, present

cr / fr / gr — crab, cry, fridge, fruit, grass, green

Phonics

dr tr	draw 	drink 	dry 	train 	tram 	tree 

sc sk	scarf 	score 	Scout 	skate 	skirt 	sky 

sm sn	small 	smell 	smooth 	snake 	snore 	snow 

sp st	speak 	spell 	sports 	stand 	star 	stop 

Dictionary

 sw

swan
sweat
sweep
sweet
swim
swing

 tw

twelfth
twelve
twice
twins
twist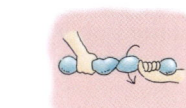
twenty

 qu

queen
quick
quiet
quiz
quarter
question

 c
 g

center
circle
cycle
ca**g**e
ju**dg**e
gin**g**er

44

Published by
Pearson Longman Asia ELT
20/F Cornwall House
Taikoo Place
979 King's Road
Quarry Bay
Hong Kong

fax: +852 2856 9578
email: pearsonlongman.hk@pearson.com
www.pearsonlongman.com

and Associated Companies throughout the world.

© Pearson Education Asia Limited 2004

All rights reserved; no part of this publication may be reproduced, stored in a retrieval system, or transmitted in any form or by any means, electronic, mechanical, photocopying, recording or otherwise, without the prior written permission of the Publishers.

First published 2002

This American English Edition first published 2004
Reprinted 2012

Produced by Pearson Education Asia Limited, Hong Kong
SWTC/ 20

ISBN-13: 978-962-00-5462-4
ISBN-10: 962-00-5462-8